For Arthur and Julie

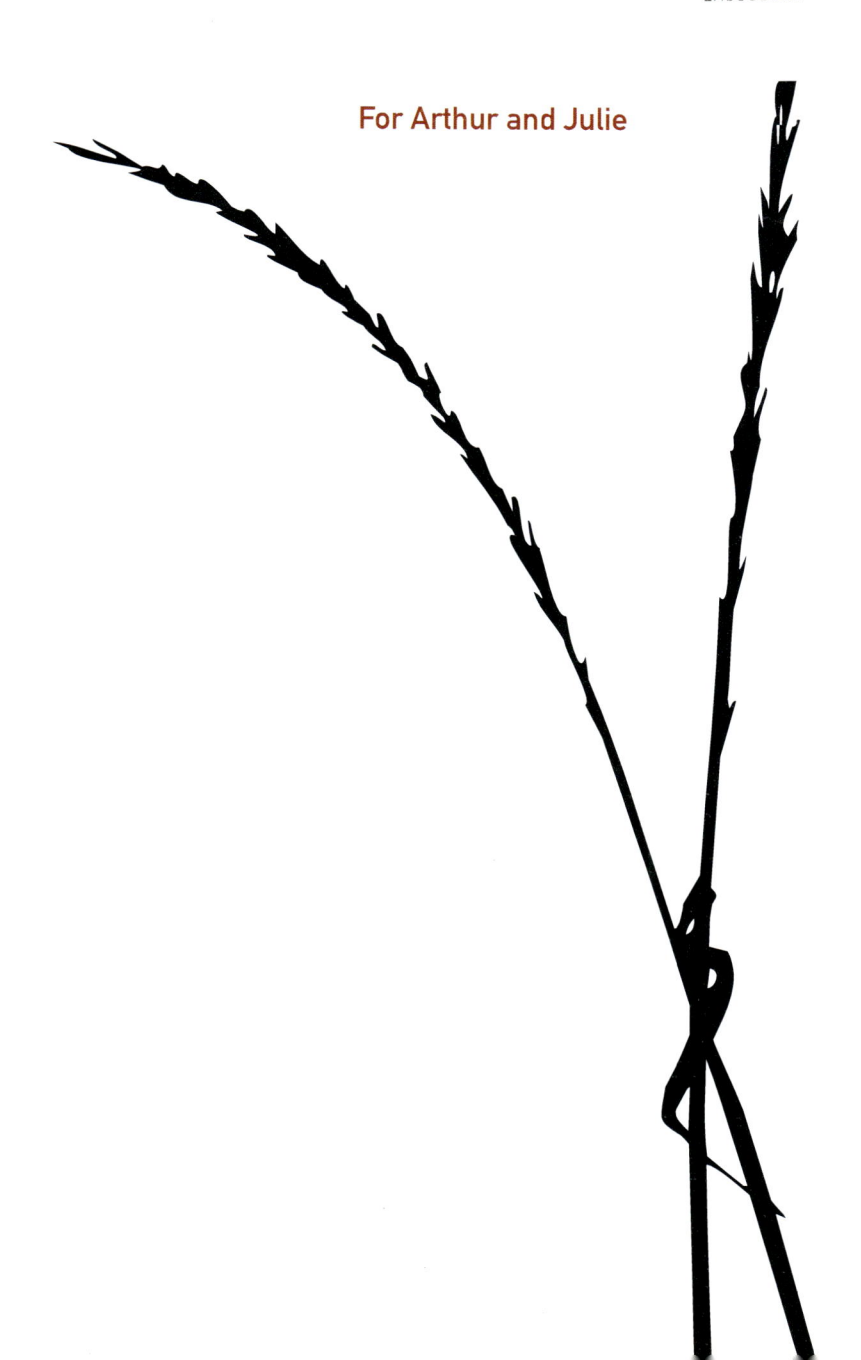

First published 2007 by Cub Publishing
Banks' Mill, 71 Bridge Street, Derby DE1 3LB.
www.cubpublishing.com

ISBN 978-0-9558017-0-9

Editorial material copyright © Jo Bell 2007

The acknowledgements on the final page constitute an extension of this copyright page.

The rights of Jo Bell and Arthur Gardner as editors,
and the individual poets as authors of their work has been asserted by them
in accordance with the Copyright, Designs and Patents Act 1988.

All rights reserved. No part of this publication may be
reproduced, stored in or introduced into a retrieval system, or
transmitted, in any form, or by any means (electronic, mechanical,
photocopying, recording or otherwise) without the prior written
permission of the publisher. Any person who does any unauthorised
act in relation to this publication may be liable to criminal
prosecution and civil claims for damages.

Typeset by Cub Publishing
Printed in Great Britain by Colourstream Ltd, Derby.

This book is sold subject to the condition that it shall not,
by way of trade or otherwise, be lent, re-sold, hired out,
or otherwise circulated without the publisher's prior consent
in any form of binding or cover other than that in which
it is published and without a similar condition including this
condition being imposed on the subsequent purchaser.

Foreword

This book came about through the diagnosis of a friend and fellow poet, Arthur Gardner, with motor neurone disease.

Like all those who meet the disease at second hand, his friends felt helpless and frustrated that they could not offer any positive relief. Those of us who first met Arthur on an Arvon course in 2001 had continued our friendship by exchanging poems and comments, and we discussed what we might do. Andrew Bailey, sometime Poetry Society staff member, immediately suggested a collection of poetry to raise money for the MND Association. Together with Derek Adams, co-organiser of the Essex Poetry Festival, we sent out a plea to poets across the UK. We offered no payment, just gratitude and a chance to help. We decided early on that the theme would not be death but life: more precisely, those landmarks large or small that stick out in our minds as we look back on life so far.

The world of published poets is a small one. In a sort of poetic twilight barking, our first contacts passed it on to theirs. Within a week we had on board some of the biggest names in contemporary poetry, and a quote from the poet laureate. Thirty six fine poets rallied to our call, giving freely the work that you read here. They wrote about birth and stillbirth; marriage and birthdays; broken love affairs and triumphant anniversaries. They are ordered alphabetically, without egos and with no attempt to impose a structure. Life is apt to throw up these events in unexpected order, as all who are affected by MND will know.

We are deeply grateful to those who have contributed poems, to the publishers who gave permission and waived fees, and hope they will agree that this book is a very worthwhile result.

It was collated by Andrew Bailey, Derek Adams, Arthur Gardner and myself, designed and printed by Cub Publishing, and edited by me and Arthur – who also paid for the print run. Wherever this book is sold, all its profits go to the Motor Neurone Disease Assocation.

Jo Bell
Co-ordinator, National Poetry Day
December 2007

Brownie Six-20 F
Derek Adams

Hold it like this says Dad
then hands me the box,
its light brown leatherette surface,
a thin skin, organic,
alive to my fingertips.
He points to a deep ruby port hole
Turn the knob till a number appears
I do and it does.
Now look in here

and that is when it happens;
the small, convex, rectangular finder
is a magic prism, Alice's looking glass,
a window to frame another world:
turn chaos to order, select patterns,
define light and shadow.
And when you are ready press here
a dull click that echoes in my head
as the final piece falls into place,
in my hands I have a Tardis
that traps light, space and time.

Going to the Chapel
Andrew Bailey

the big intended *and* impending and no fear
though films insist, no vault instead
with exultation over sofa, oh my stated other
oh my same, with heart as willing here's
all intimate in intended memories my hand

lovely and loving and loved and in reverence
before one another, at least I before you, you
have with your *yes* kicked off a teleology
so, though so much done, so however much,
is still no dent in the set of all things to do

and *all* done without you counts now
undone, can never do everything, no, but can leap
in intent on everything shrinking and small
as is possible, smaller and smaller and
small as we can and what's next?

Watershed
Jo Bell

The source is odd, coming to it as we do at close of day.
A hand-held scramble over bog and hedgehog grass;
then silence. Wetness. Nothing mystical, we say
and hurry darkly to the car, owls hooting shapeless in the woods.

Hours on, I'm smoothing maps beneath a Green Man in the guest-house beam.
You watch your river hunch and stretch across the page,
and mark the point where summer set us floating. I remember
twilight herons, glass-eels throwing slip-knots in the bulrush roots.

On that first journey, we ate peaches as we steered. The river sniffed
at sedge and vetch, and dawdled at the bank then quietly pushed on,
stubborn in its deeper channels. Your long fingers touched the tiller.
In the cabin, I smelt peach and diesel on your skin.

Still mapping, now you chart the winter Sunday where the Bore came
like a muscle moving up, a swallow in the river's throat:
oystercatchers scattering, like crumbs from shaken cloth. You all pride
and wonder, humbled as the glass ribs pushed unknowing past.

Last, your finger traces broader water at your present mooring,
twelve miles from your childhood. Docked in the Severn's thickest coil,
strong as whipcord or a mother's love. Living now by building boats,
learning at the river's knee. Gulls scrying through the spars above.

You stretch your spine away, to look across the masts.
A river's for travelling on, you say.

Porthgwarra
Charles Bennett

Sit with me here at Porthgwarra,
let's listen to the bell in the buoy
and notice the way whatever we hadn't noticed
is coming to rest in a greeny-blue interval
between the strike of one sour sea-note and
the next. And even if it's true that the voice
in the buoy is the groan of a drowning man,
after a while the sunlight will warm these stones,
and the day swing round by itself
on the right heading. So let's sit quietly here
while everything falls into place. And then
when we speak, let's speak at the same time
and state the obvious: *This is the life,* we'll say
and yes, it will be.

Bracebridge

For Lucy
Julie Boden

Pushed out like a sleigh one May morning.
The dry land would not carry you.
In the stillness of your birth
my heart felt the coming of winter.

Since then, each year, as snowdrops bow
and laughter sings between the trees
I walk the Bracebridge walk beside the lake
that helps, somehow.

In Derbyshire, upon those stepping stones,
we waved your ashes back to find the sea
then walked beneath a sky of piercing blue
to offer up your white cloud memory.

If, in the tiny promise of a life…
if parts of you have helped another live
then there is something else that we can bless.

Only, let them hear the music of your birth,
the music tiny organs might have played
before they take the knife.

Lying in Grass
Mandy Coe

Above us, a loch of sky
framed in grass. Grasshoppers leap
from bank to bank.

The air is full of noise and golden
light blesses our skin with sheen.
Her hair, cool and dark, curtains it all

as we bend close
to finger little white buttons
undone – or done up, depending

where the memory starts.

Heron in the Alyn
Gladys Mary Coles

I follow the river, heron-seeking
where weed and nettle reign,
caught in my sorrows
and my imagined sorrows.
Flies flick and rise, torment
slow cattle. Willows trail the water
and floating celandine; maybe also Ophelia
singing *'O, you must wear your rue*
with a difference.'

Seeking the heron
I make unexpected finds -
the sludge of a water-rat's lair,
sheep's wool a ragged veil on wire,
a tree-wound colonised by fungus –
and suddenly I see the secret bird!

Hidden in a tanglebend
grey visitant in fish-vigil,
alert in the afternoon heat.
Such startled lift-off
of great wings, crashing
through boughs, attaining sky.

I watch the slow pulse
of its flight, the laboured ease,
diminishing into distance
with its weight of unseen freight –
my sorrows, my imagined sorrows.

Possibility
Julia Copus

Some days feel a budding in their stems,
an itch in the skin of things:
walls soften; a chair becomes lissom,
acquiring a suppleness in its frame;
a book, straight-backed and serious,
takes to the air; and the carpet
shifts and loosens on its sea-bed.
On such days it is down to us
whether we wait for things to pass
or manage, with a simple gesture,
to inslide ourselves, cut loose, set sail –
vessels of the possible.

Wayzgoose*
Jane Draycott

Waist-high the wheat is talking, the great
conversation. We motor past, foreheads
to the glass, and climb through hedgerow
margins to the edge of the known world.

On the hill's broad back, offered like snow
without a sound, we now lay out
the argument and patterning of our feast.

Where we have come, summer applies
its even weight to tarmac, cornfields
and the silent lake where no ink lies.

Where we are going, the goose has
in her eye and takes her onward flight,
nib-neck leading toward the season
of quiet work by candlelight.

*annual excursion for printing employees, traditionally August 24th (St .Bartholomew's Eve)

Another Poem About Old Photographs
Ian Duhig

This one's good. Look closely, you can almost
detect each ridge and whorl of Uncle Tommy's index-
fingerprint. That white curved edge top left – that's
the sky we had in Cork, Nineteen Fifty-Six,
the summer of his first box camera. This one
I call 'Early Malevich: Town Hall, Macroom'
or, if in a figurative whimsy, 'Klansmen
Routed by Doves in Freak Arkansas Snowstorm.'
It should have been the family group
but Tommy was, by then, flouting convention.
Drunk with Kodakry, he'd wave us round, then swoop -
Duhigs trapped between his cross-sights and the sun,
the Red-faced Baron, hunched behind a black box
which struggled to record his flights or art
on sun-bleached or thumb-benighted film. This next
came out. My mother couldn't believe it.
Plain as sin, my father's Harris blocks the view
to Gougane Barra from Glengariff Bay.
"The best jacket I ever had," he'd say,
"no doubt about it. The camera doesn't lie."

An Interior
Paul Farley

They ask why I still bother coming back.
London must be great this time of year.
I'm not listening. My eyes have found
the draining-board, its dull mineral shine,
the spice rack, still exactly how I left it,
knives, a Vermeer vinyl table-mat.
How many hours did I spend watching
the woman pouring milk into a bowl
that never fills? I never tired of it.
Vision persists, doesn't admit the breaks
the artist must have taken, leg-stretching
alongside a canal twitching with sky
not unlike the leaden one outside;
or just leant on the door jamb, looking out
onto a courtyard, smoking a pipe
before going in, to sleep on his excitement.

Equinox
Leah Fritz

As the curtain erratically begins
to open on the bright proscenium
of spring, I notice that during the winter some
small changes have been made on set, and sense
a subtle disparity in ambience –
new growth of trees above last summer's height,
and younger magpies (though still black and white,
they look the same), building new nests, scavenge
among the secret topmost leaves. All this
I see, as in the mirror I make up
my not-so-subtly altered face; take up,
let out the suit that only last year fit
me well enough, and step into the light
of longer days – almost the same, not quite.

Fledging
Anne-Marie Fyfe

Little bird – the midwife sighed
handing me a cooing daughter
with a wren-like heartbeat.
Downy wisps trimmed her ears.
Weeks before I noticed
the wings. Tiny harp-shaped scales
nestled in shoulderblades. A gift.

She slept those first winter months
on quilted eider, wakened,
spring days, to birdsong,
twitched infant wings for size.
I heaped mattresses and bolsters
for first flutters from the coalshed,
fed her cod-liver oil and mango,
dried pumpkin-seeds for her lunch-pack.
She grew more sleek with seasons.

Nightly I see her cross landmasses,
oceans, take snow-powdered sierras
in her migratory path, always
on some or other summit, fledging.

Circus-Apprentice
Katherine Gallagher

I'm learning it all – acrobatics, clowning,
riding bareback and trapeze,
fire from a sleeve: my hand's a wand.

I weave my life round dancing elephants
who spray the air while turning
their backs on the crowd;

lions who never put a foot wrong.
I'm taking their cue, I've seen
what people want.

Prancing ponies teach me steps:
pacing, adroitness, like my fellow-dancers
keeping their spot.

I'm walking the high-wire, making my mark
poised, balanced, don't look away –
you are my gravity's other edge.

Blessings
Arthur Gardner

Sleeping, as we do, with the curtains open
the sun, moon and stars peer in
even Orion drops by without being invited.

Sleeping, as we do, with the windows open
the sounds of trains, planes and cars pour in
they all seem delighted.

We had not expected such attention.
We had not meant to put ourselves on show.
We merely thought to take and hold what we found good
and let all others go.

How to Begin a Person
Rosie Garner

Take a night when the canvas rips,
where something stumbles outside in the dark
and plastic chairs somersault in sheeting rain
snagged by windbreak beech, the field's edge.

A night in which, in any case,
you would not have slept,
when you were pushing wet feet into boots
to check guy ropes, hammer in pegs,
soaked in seconds and back inside
for a shuddering cup of red wine
hours and hours after the headlong dash
from pub to tent.

So it's a seduction of sorts,
an unguarding under the rocking light.
Odd glimpses of knee and belly,
rain wet hair, the concertinaing of sleeping bags.

In the morning we rest on the beach
the storm's memory a fidget in the waves
You are laid out on rocks, heavy with hangover,
I am lying on the sea's soft edge dreaming of Zeus
rushing down in a shower of light
changing to restless sea water.
And in that moment, the beginnings of a child
who will always be
the calm beyond the storm.

At Fourteen, P.A. to the Managing Director
Roz Goddard

Oh, you'll be something all right
My father said as we sped
to an industry do in his oily van,
the footwell littered with pictures of compressors
and other tools for powering the world.
Ah, no one knows the glamour of Plant Hire.

Today, you are P.A. to the Managing Director
I would be. I had the badge.
Me hardly fourteen, P.A. to a Midas man
sliding in his gilded footsteps as one deal after
another was sealed, running for egg sandwiches,
tapping giants on the sleeve, asking for cards.

My most trusted lieutenant, don't let me down.
As if. That day I could have been profiled
in the trade mag, the whiz kid taking Plant Hire
by storm. I'd be the short one in the 'How we Met'
column. The crown of her head was cresting the world,
when I spotted her potential, would be his quote.
He walks me through this world of men, I can do anything,
would be mine.

Letter of Resignation
Cathy Grindrod

Dear Sir

Stuff your

recycling bins, map-pins, win-wins, acronyms, your post-tray, in-tray, out-tray,

up-yours tray, your 2-finger kit kats, mouse mat (sit on that).

Keep your

four-wheel drive, A drive, C drive, sex-drive, shared disks, compact disks,

floppy disks, flaccid disks, minicom, CD Rom, dot com, monk on, www dot,

bald spot, brain (not).

Buy your own

duplex, ofrex, tippex, semtex, skreenkleen, caffeine, windolene, guillotine,

flora lite, megabyte, load a shite web site.

I'm out of here, no fear, fifth gear, way clear.

Enjoy your

hair dyed, bit on the side, hotel guide, quick ride.

When I said I had saved all the records

I lied.

Dancer
A F Harrold

She dances lightly,
to heavy music,
some in her head,
some in the air
and leaves a flickering
flower with those
few who watch
but who don't join in.

Grace isn't given
to everyone,
and at times freedom
is hard to value.
I watch and watch,
aware of her,
but aware of myself
more – I don't dance.

And Let Us Say
(for Emma McKiernan, on her birth, 8/9/99)
Matthew Hollis

That if the linen flapped too loud
The washing line was taken down

And if a shopdoor bell was rung
Its tongue was held with cotton thumbs

And if a milkfloat tattled by
It was flagged down and held aside

And should the rivers drown us out
We had them dammed at every mouth

And coughed our engines gently off
And wrapped our tyres in woollen socks

And sat awhile on silent roads
Or dawdled home in slippered shoes

And did not sound but held our tongues
And watched our watches stop, and startle on.

Miniatures (iii)
Chris Jones

You barely remember those first three months
but now each day's all memory
since you map his skin's spray of freckles
and watch his blonde hairs blow auburn.

Already a first language has been lost
as the coastline of his ears unfolds,
and those milk-sweet stools that flecked your days
leave you like the smell of gloves from fingers.

Today the watermarks of his nipples,
the knuckle-buds and dimples of his fists:
you learn his body's tender reaches
just as he out-leaps you again.

Return to Edgeley Park
John Lindley

It takes me back:
that familiar turnstile creak,
the smell of piss
on the dark splashed walls of the Gents,
the rain made special by floodlight.
We've done all this before, Dad, years ago
before arthritis got your legs
and a miserly muse got my attention.
Those days you'd stand in the paddock
instead of limping to your seat in the stand.
Those days I could let the smell
of your tobacco drift across my face
without writing a sodding poem about it.

Two Mugs
Allison MacVety

Corned beef chunks and tinned spaghetti
heated over a primus stove on the concrete floor
of our new home. The cistern's blocked, there's no

power and someone's filched the door handles.
We have a mattress, a toothbrush, the two mugs
we fetched south with us in a banged-up wreck.

Tomorrow the removals van will bring the rest,
but tonight, you say, *it'll never be better than this,*
your breath a white noise fuzzing the sharp air.

Solo
Esther Morgan

She takes nothing with her
but the crows' feet
round her eyes,
the white ring of skin
on her naked finger.

All down the long avenue of pines
her headlights lift
each tree into place
like the ripple of arms
in a *corps de ballet.*

as the swan passes.

Killing Time
Ruth O'Callaghan

When the letter came she took a small knife
to the faded forsythia that had once thrust
deep yellow against their windows.

For his chemotherapy he refused
her offer of a lift leaving her bent
over shrivelled daffs, binding them tightly.

Waiting, she cut dahlias, divided tubers,
scraped scales from lily bulbs
but at the thought of propagation

discarded them. The day of his operation
she made incisions in pliable stems,
stripped side shoots, tore at petals. To kill time

she hacked two flowering yew branches
which obscured the view of the river.

Forty Years On
Harry Owen

How an hour stays forever: down this
back staircase in the rich darkness of Wales,
a silver river singing outside, air

filled with moss and foreign grasses, and I
bear my heart to the door like a boulder,
erratic and massive as mountainsides.

You are something without me, cool and clean,
a crystal devil-gift beneath the night sky
as we walk (go on! go on!) these half-turned
shoulders of hills, the kingdoms of the world.

Inviolate as a new planet, lost,
forbidden, you hover there like a moon,
this moment truer than my face, my hand.

For I loved you then, I loved you then. Still do.

Remembrance of an Open Wound
after Frida Kahlo
Pascale Petit

Whenever we make love, you say
it's like making love to a crash –
I bring the bus with me into the bedroom.
There's a lull, like before the fire brigade
arrives, flames licking the soles
of our feet. Neither of us knows
when the petrol tank will explode.
You say I've decorated my house
to recreate the accident –
my skeleton wired with fireworks,
my menagerie flinging air about.
You look at me in my gold underwear –
a crone of sixteen, who lost
her virginity to a lightning bolt.
It's time to pull the handrail out.
I didn't expect love to feel like this –
you holding me down with your knee,
wrenching the steel rod from my charred body
quickly, kindly, setting me free.

On Emerald Downs
Diana Pooley

'A wigwam for a goose's bridle,'
Grandpa Copland said
every time I asked what something was.
And he called me Nanny.
When I asked him why, he'd say,
'It's short for nanny goat'.
Grandma Copland called me Posy,
did my hair in bunches and sang to us
'Way down upon the Swanee River'
and knew by heart two pages
of 'The Song of Hiawatha'.

Why I Lost my Virginity
Pauline Rowe

Because we played Little Women at home.
Because I was never allowed to be Jo.
Because my father slept in the shed.
Because my mother went to college.
Because I first read Blake when I was six.
Because my father had no O-levels.

Because we laughed at Britten's Oberon.
Because his painted flesh was huge.
Because his high voice made me think of school.
Because your friend "simply adored Ferlinghetti".
Because I had to leave the table.
Because I had to hide away to laugh.

Because the wine was warm.
Because the conversation was low.
Because the eating of a paid-for meal was new.
Because I was dazzled by desire.
Because it was snowing and the fire was warm.
Because the lamp was lit, the room was safe.

Because the noise at home became too loud.
Because I was foolish, vain, unloved.
Because you were certain, gentle, funny.
Because your marriage was in tatters.
Because you knew what to do.
Because you needed to.

Because you told me I was everything.
Because I knew I was nothing.
Because I had a taste for it.

Because life is too short.
Because I was too short.
Because I was fifteen.

This is how it will be
Andrew Rudd

You will open your eyes
in the morning, and the world
will run to you in its best suit.

Trees will make shadow-plays
with their fingers. Creatures
will call out their names.

You will open your ears to music
no-one has heard before, voices of those
you love and those who love you,

the highest note and the deep note
which is only a stirring in the earth. You will
open your mouth, and the things you say

will be old words in new shapes.
Your stories will weave all the threads
into one cloth. You will open

your hand, scatter bread for birds,
give to those who have nothing to give.
Your hand will take hold of another hand

and walk into a new world,
which is your world, and our world, and we
will be behind you.

Chapel, Women's Hospital
Sibyl Ruth

When you left the two of us
on that first day

the child breathed at my side
in her clear box.
A new work on display.

Before driving home
you walked down a corridor
into a plain room

where dry flowers bloomed in a vase.
There were three rows of chairs,
one opened book in a case
with a list of names.

Many more than you could hold or touch.

The record of those
whose boxes had been put away
sealed up.

And you knew we had done nothing.
Nothing to deserve
the size, the shape, the sheer weight of our luck.

Blood rang in your ears.
Your neck tightened.
Words could not be enough.

But prayer surged at your throat.
It cried out. You said
Thanks.

Thank you very much.

Reading My Son
Catherine Smith

His last school day; he strolls in through the door,
his shirt signed in fat felt-tips by his mates.
Sophie loves him loads and Todd reminds him
to keep in touch by nightly MSN.
Jodie's going to miss his wicked laugh.
Mel rates his hair and someone wants his babies.

I try to read him. He drinks orange juice
straight from the carton, towering over me.
He's going out tonight. He turns the bass up.
The shirt's sloughed off. I'll hold it once he's gone.

Veress
Todd Swift

Bicycling along the Danube,
Summer's breadth before us.

The river runs past, islands, bathers.
Sometimes we're on a crowded path

And other times, only closed factories
Or newly-planted trees. The motion,

The ease of this, alive in this artifice
Of lush composing green, not unlike

June flashing onto spokes and skin.
Each reflection, combined in the eye

That oversees the ephemeral given
Thinks: this is joy, this is a good day.

That private angel in our heart's lens
Collects such imaged quickness,

Keeps and spreads it out.
Your shout, as you came upon a hill

Letting both pedals go,
Finding their own too-fast revolutions

In descent, while I, seconds behind,
Had no idea what your cry meant.

First Love
Colin Watts

Nurse Flynn had a blue and white uniform
that looked smooth, but felt rough.
She smelt of ether and told me
a rabbit needed its appendix
to get rid of the chlorophyll, but I didn't,
so not to be worrying
and would I get on and eat up my cabbage.

I was clamped with clips like those I fitted
to the axles of Meccano lorries to keep the wheels on.
I dared not strain on the bedpan in case I split open.
Nurse Flynn told me the clips were safe
as the Bank of Ireland. And anyways,
hadn't I been stitched up also with Connemara cotton,
the strongest in the whole world:
wasn't I the best belt and braces job she'd ever seen?

I liked the men's ward, especially the farting.
Mr Johnson taught me to tell the time.
'When the big hand gets to the twelve,'
he said, 'and the little one to the four,
your mum and dad will come.' I wanted them
to bring my two baby sisters, but I had to make do
with three Rupert annuals and a box of pineapple tarts.

Nurse Flynn brought me breakfast, lunch and tea
and took me for sun-ray treatment.
The rubber strap on the dark goggles
pinched my ears and smelt like our bath-mat.
I cried when it was time to go home
and asked Nurse Flynn if she would marry me.
She said it would be her pleasure
but she'd have to ask her Daddy first.

Dancing to the Tune
Joy Winkler

The ribbon's taut as we make our last under.
Boys in billowing white shirts, girls in blue
are patterned tightly round the maypole, true
to pagan ritual. Have they made a blunder
this Church of England school? It's a wonder
that there is no bolt of lightning due
as we turn around, determined to unscrew
the plaited good luck charm. Not even thunder
remonstrates our gesture to the phallus
as in and out we weave to jolly tunes
to entertain our orbed and prinked May Queen.
And not one of our righteous teachers tell us
that these are actions close linked to the moon.
Thank goodness the unravelling comes out clean.

Landmark
Peter Wyton

I shall buy a chalk hillside,
Carve you into an Eighth Wonder,
Taller than the Cerne Giant,
If somewhat less explicit,
Though your contours will be laid bare
To this and to future generations.

When the outline of your head
Is visible three counties away,
Some bureaucratic backlash
Will undoubtedly occur.
Officialdom may pounce while I'm
Scrimshawing round your shoulders.

I will persist in sculpting
Your torso, despite sorties by
Aircraft from the militant wing
Of the Countryside Commission.
Women's groups and po-faced bishops
Will criticise the acreage of your breasts.

Some scrap of modesty *will*
Be required, in case lewd persons
Take you for a fertility symbol.
I can't have couples abseiling
Down your cleavage, for the pleasure
Of procreating in your navel.

I shall draw a discreet vale
Of vegetation across your
Lower slopes, indicating
To future historians the deep
Social significance of
The twentieth century mini-skirt.

By the time our grand-children
Have populated the planets,
You will be legendary.
Clear cut beacon of mother earth,
Folk from remote galaxies will
Navigate to your outstretched arms.

Acknowledgements

All reproduced by kind permission of the publisher.

Possibility Julia Copus
from *In Defence of Adultery* (Bloodaxe Books, 2003)

An Interior Paul Farley
from *The Ice Age* (Picador, 2002)

Fledging Anne-Marie Fyfe
from *Tickets for a Blank Window* (Rockingham Press, 2002)

Circus-Apprentice Katherine Gallagher
from *Circus-Apprentice* (Arc Publications, 2002)

And Let Us Say Matthew Hollis
from *Ground Water* (Bloodaxe Books, 2004)

Remembrance of an Open Wound *after Frida Kahlo* Pascale Petit
from *The Wounded Deer - Fourteen poems after Frida Kahlo* (Smith/Doorstop, 2005)

© All poems remain copyright of the individual writers.